Out There

Written by Christina He

Illustrated by Milind Setn

Consonant Ll /l/	Consonant Nn /n/	Consonant Rr /r/	Consonant Zz /z/
last	not	run	zip
like	run		

High-Frequency Words

all	here	so	what
do	into	then	
have	out	there	

1

What is that out there?

It is white and wet.
It is not hot at all.

Zip up so we do not get wet.

Get a cap on top.
Then we can go out.

We like to make piles.

Then we run and jump in the piles.
We like to play out here.

We want it to last.
It is so fun!